*Edu-K for KIDs!

by

Paul E. Dennison, Ph.D.
&
Gail E. Dennison

* The basic manual on Educational Kinesiology for parents & teachers of Kids of all ages!

Published by
Edu-Kinesthetics, Inc.
Post Office Box 3396
Ventura, CA 93006-3396
U.S.A.

ISBN—0-942143-01-9

A MESSAGE TO PARENTS AND EDUCATORS:

EDUCATIONAL KINESIOLOGY FOR KIDS is the long awaited sequel to SWITCHING ON by Dr. Paul E. Dennison which was first published in 1981. EDUCATIONAL KINESIOLOGY FOR KIDS is not a children's book. It is a book for parents and teachers to read and use with children to help them to better understand how they learn or block learning at school. When children understand the relationship of the brain and the body, they are more open to the changes made possible by this work.

EDU-K FOR KIDS is an illustrated, self-explanatory approach to a complex issue. It is intended to explain brain function as it relates to specific learning tasks. Each page on the brain captures a moment in time in the life of Tim as he deals with the trials of learning to read, write, and spell. Liberties have been taken to simplify a mystifying process. Everything which is depicted is neurologically correct; however, "switching off" is relative to the individual and the situation. The illustrations are to suggest only the need for better hemispheric integration.

The Brain Gym® activities taught in this book are safe, simple, natural movements which the homolateral, one-sided learner will tend to avoid doing unless given your permission and encouragement. As children and adults become better integrated, they want more of these exercises and quickly include them in their daily lives. They have proven successful in promoting a more integrated use of the eyes, ears, and body for improved reading, writing, and spelling. In fact, not only school subjects, but all activities improve with the use of Brain Gym®.

When children learn with the whole brain they are open, receptive, and curious about their environment. Simultaneously, they are able to express themselves, make new experiences their own, and be aware of their own uniqueness. This is our goal for every person on the planet.

Paul E. Dennison, Ph.D.
Gail Dennison
November, 1984

Dedicated to our children,
Who continuously teach us
the joyful connection between
learning & spontaneous movement!

TABLE OF CONTENTS

NOTES

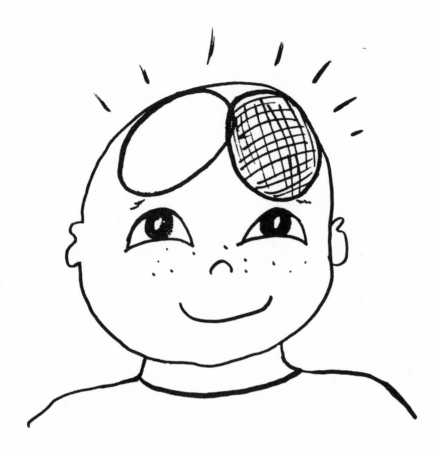

Hi, I'm Tim. I used to have difficulties learning new things, no matter how hard I tried. Then I met Eddy. He taught me Brain Gym. Now I know how to learn!

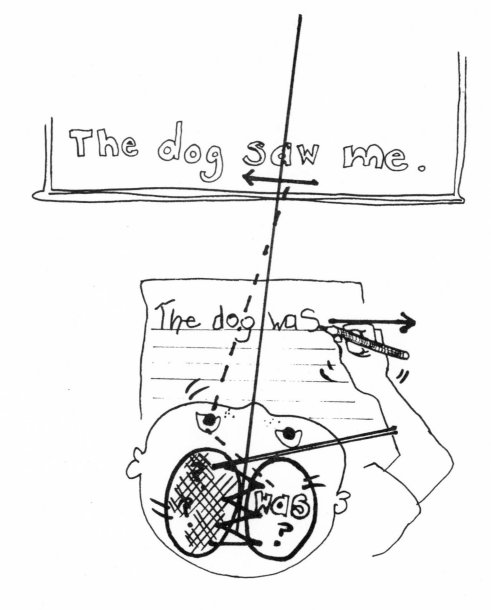

TIM IS REPATTERNED

← This was me at school. I was always confused. Often my eye would go one way while my hand went the other, without me even knowing it! When I made mistakes like this, I felt dumb. I was not using my two brains together.

One day a new teacher came to our school. His name was Eddy.

Eddy said he would do Brain Gym® with me!

Eddy said that Brain Gym® would help me read and learn better.

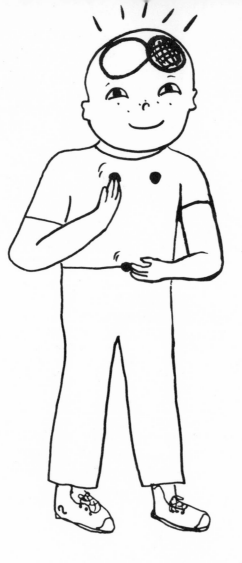

Brain Buttons

Before Eddy checked my muscles, he told me to press my "brain buttons" by rubbing below my collarbone while holding my navel. I felt more alert!

Cooks Hook-ups

Before Eddy checked me, he said to sit for one minute with my body in an 8. Then he said to sit with my finger tips together for another minute. I took a deep breath with my tongue on the roof of my mouth. I felt ready to learn.

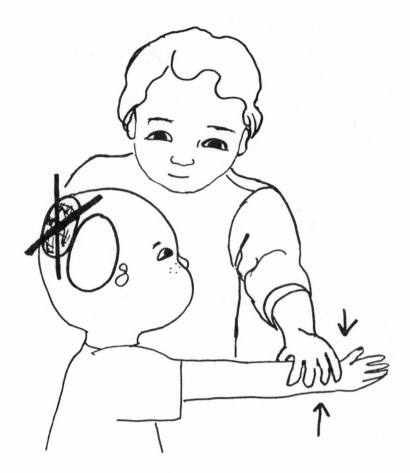

"Let's do an experiment," suggested Eddy. He told me to hold up
my arm. "Tell me when to push
gently down on your arm. Can you
hold it up against my pressure?
Do your best," he said. Eddy
could not push my arm down.
I felt capable. "You are switched on,"
he said. I liked him.

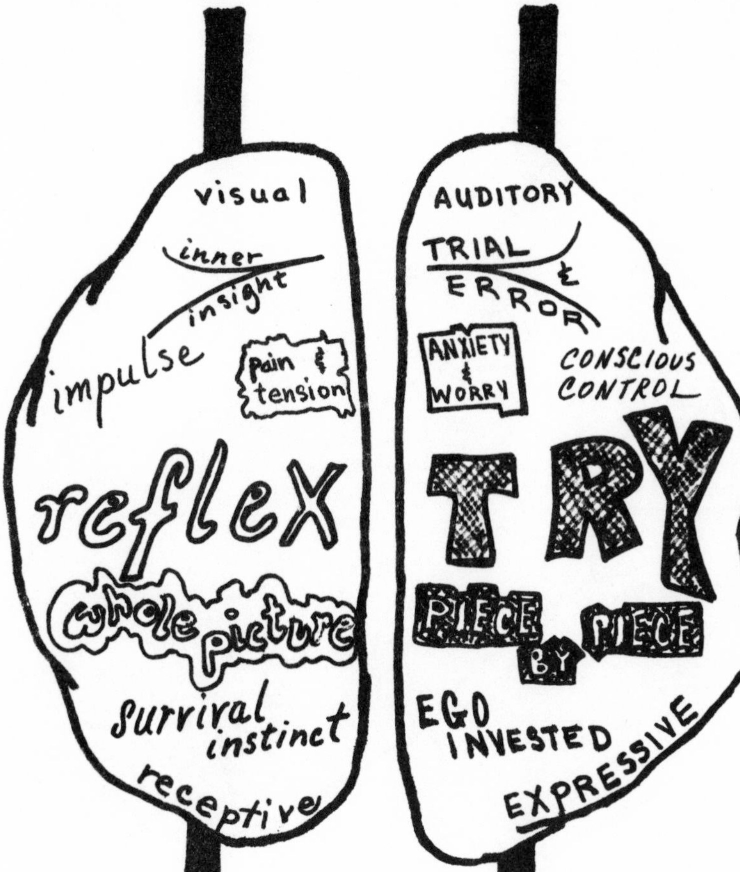

visual

inner
insight

impulse

pain &
tension

AUDITORY

TRIAL
& ERROR

ANXIETY
& WORRY

CONSCIOUS
CONTROL

reflex

TRY

whole picture

PIECE BY PIECE

survival
instinct

EGO
INVESTED

EXPRESSIVE

receptive

(This is Tim's brain as he faces you. The higher potentials of his brain are not available to him when he uses only one hemisphere at one time and "switches off" the other. Both are needed for successful learning experiences.)

7

Then Eddy asked me to "try harder." "Okay." I really tried my hardest, but my arm went right down.

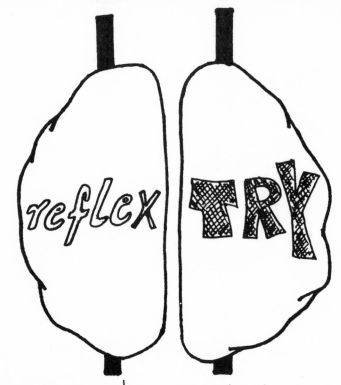

Eddy explained that I was using
my "try" brain now, instead of my
"reflex" brain. He said my "reflex"
brain would always keep me safe
and strong when I needed it!

Whenever I "try" I feel weak-
er because I "switch off" my
"reflex" brain.

When I "do my best," my
body does the right thing without "trying".

9

DENNISON LATERALITY REPATTERNING

Eddy then asked me to "cross crawl," being sure to cross the midline by touching my opposite knee. This was not easy for me. I thought I was going to fall over. He checked my muscle and I was switched off. "This activity is something which makes you <u>try</u>," Eddy explained.

"Look at this X." He checked me
and I was "switched off" again. "This
is a symbol for crossing the midline,"
explained my friend. "Right now
you must "try" whenever you get
to the midline. That is why reading
and writing are so hard.

Then Eddy asked me to do another movement which he called
the "puppet" or "one side at
a time (homolateral)" crawl. This
was so easy for me. I wished
everything at school was this
easy!

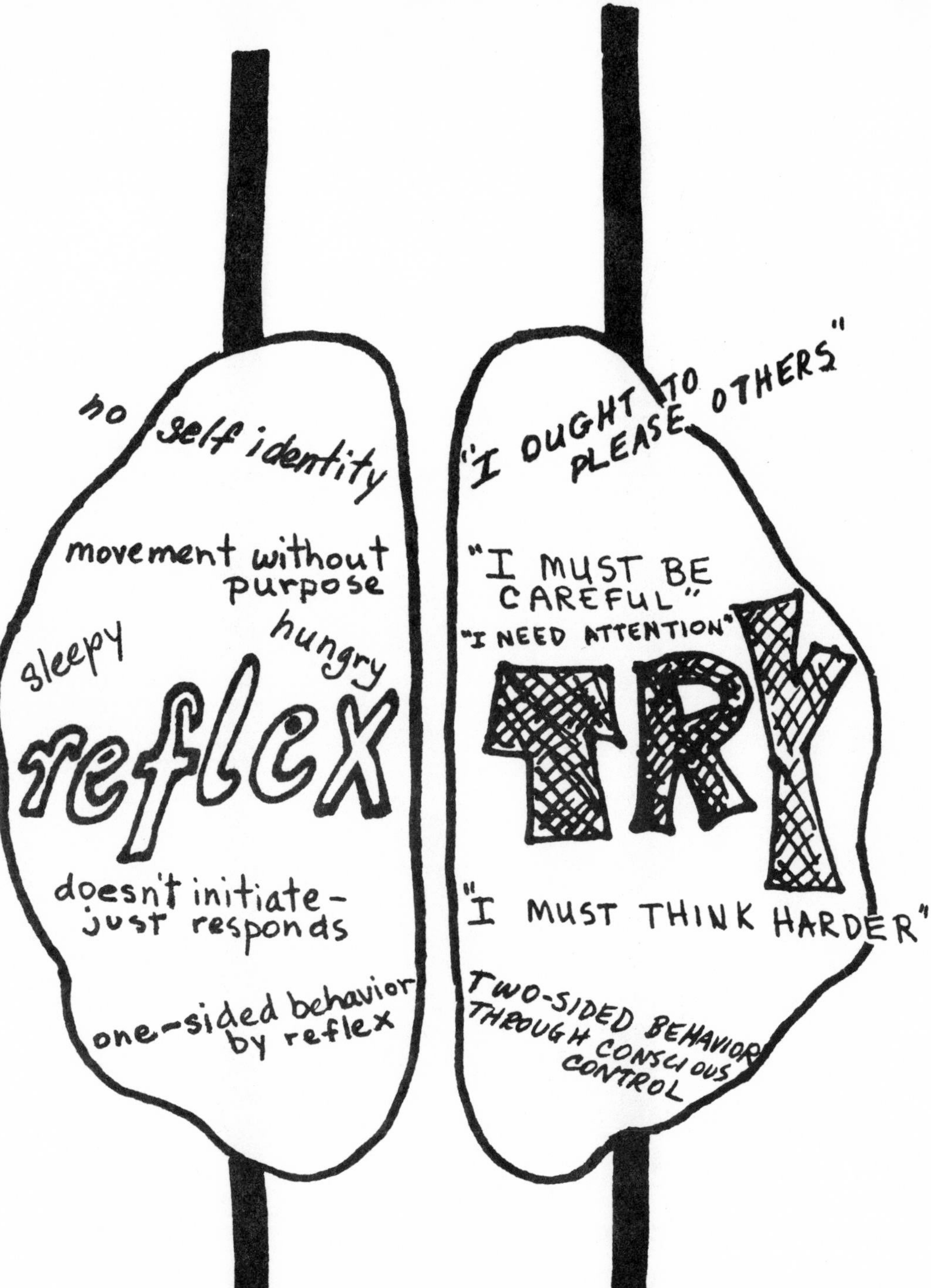

no self identity

movement without purpose

sleepy   hungry

reflex

doesn't initiate - just responds

one-sided behavior by reflex

"I OUGHT TO PLEASE OTHERS"

"I MUST BE CAREFUL"

"I NEED ATTENTION"

TRY

"I MUST THINK HARDER"

TWO-SIDED BEHAVIOR THROUGH CONSCIOUS CONTROL

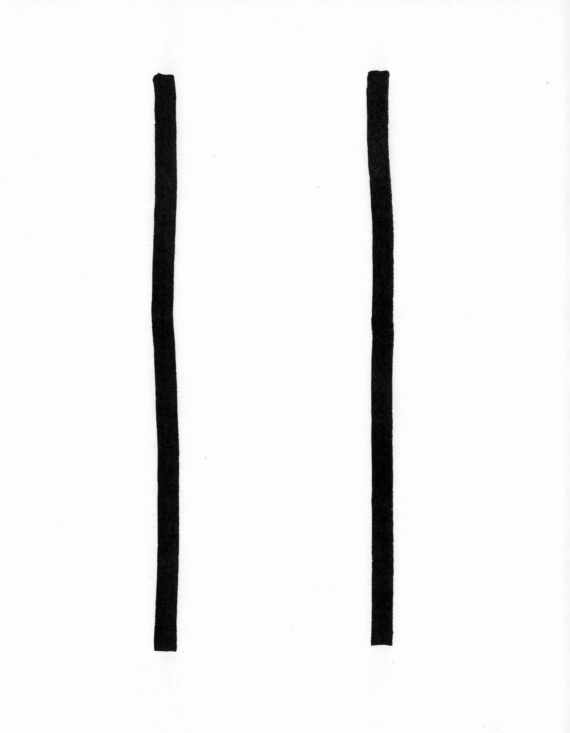

Now Eddy showed me two parallel
vertical lines. He checked me as
I looked at the lines. I became
stronger than ever. " You prefer
to work with one brain on at a
time. Your brain feels safest that
way right now," he assured.

Eddy told me how the brain and body learn to work together. "Babies who crawl enough grow up to use their 'reflex' and their 'try' brains at the same time. For people who skip the crawling stage, the two cerebral hemispheres do not seem to cooperate as well during learning."

Eddy asked if I was prepared to be repatterned so that my "reflex" brain and "try" brain would work together better, just as if I had crawled.

I said "Yes!"

He said, "Let's see if you are ready."

He stated, "This person's system is ready for repatterning," as he checked my brain response.

I was strong and ready!

Eddy smiled, "Now we know you are ready for growth."

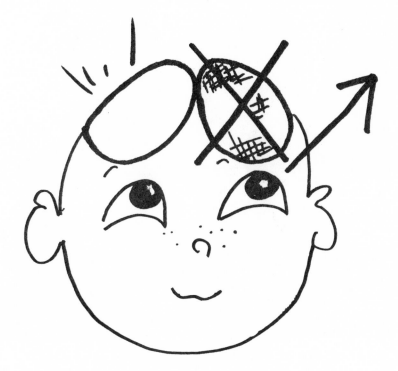

Eddy explained that most people have their "reflex" brain in the right hemisphere and the "try" in the left. To turn on my reflex brain, I just had to look up to the left.

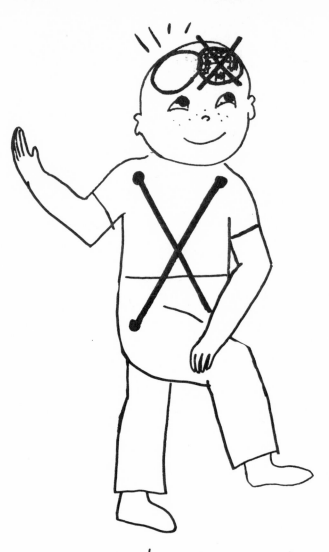

Eddy helped me to cross crawl
while I looked up to the left.
To my surprise, after the
first few steps, I could do
it easily by myself. I was
crossing the midline!

Eddy checked me again. I was
strong on cross crawling instead
of switched off. "Does this
mean I did my best and was not
trying any more?" Eddy
smiled, "Yes, it does!"

Then I did the "puppet" crawl
looking down to the right to
activate my "try" brain. This
time this movement felt awkward
and self-conscious.

Eddy checked me after the puppet crawl. Switched off! "Now your brain and body know how to stop and think when you are in new learning situations.

Eddy said that I was learning that whole body movement,
crossing the midline so that
both brain hemispheres can
cooperate, is preferable to par-
tial movement.

He asked me to clasp my hands
together tightly to imagine my
brains working together.

Eddy asked me to cross crawl looking in all directions: up, down, left, right. I didn't check weak in any direction!

"Does this mean that both sides of my brain and body want to work together automatically, as one?" I asked.

"You got it!" Eddy agreed.

Then I did the puppet crawl looking in all directions. I felt switched off and I laughed.

Eddy did the puppet crawl too. I checked him. His muscle was switched off, too!

Eddy said my body now knows the easy way to learn and will not prefer the hard way ever again.

I do not have to be repatterned again. Looking at an X or cross crawling always "switches me on!"

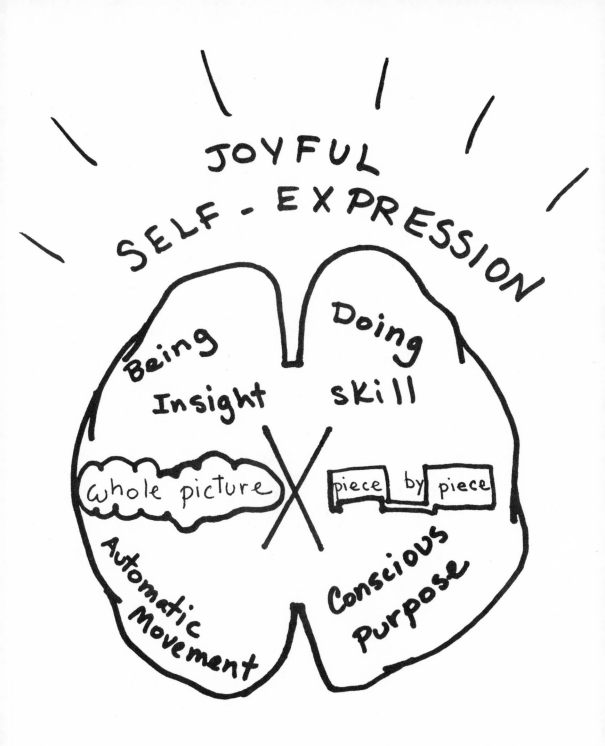

Reading across the Midline

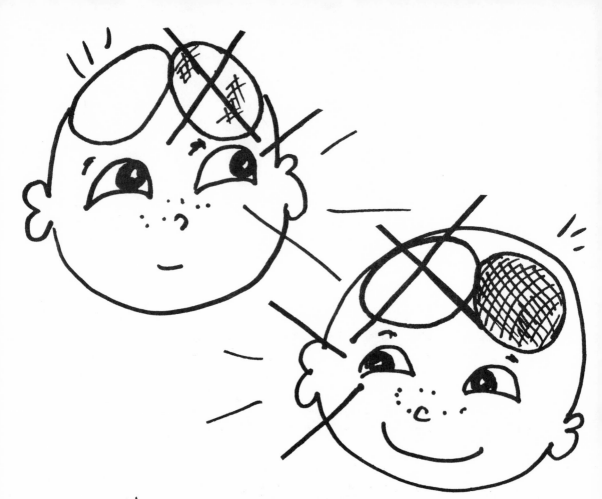

Here I am before I learned
to cross the midline for reading. When I looked to the left,
I "switched off" my "try" brain.
When I looked to the right,
I switched off my "reflex"
brain. I couldn't move my eyes
across the page very well.

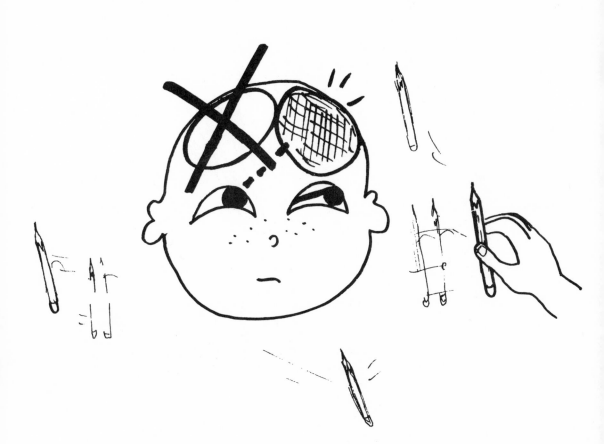

When Eddie did eye exercises
with me (called tracking) I
would "switch off" one hemisphere.
After repatterning for eyes, I
could track in all directions!

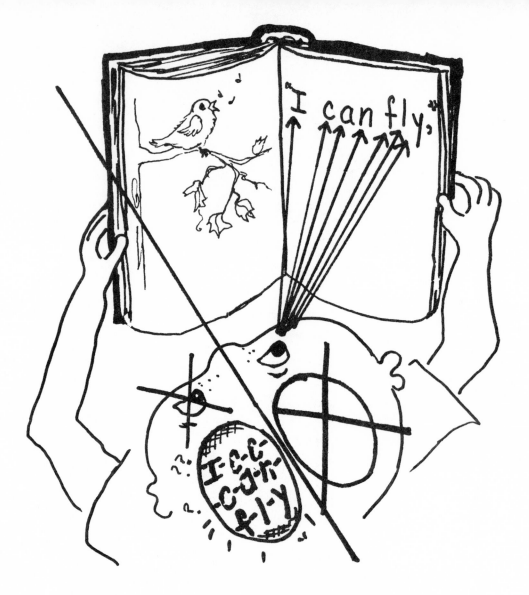

(When Tim read with his
right eye on and his left eye
off, he got lost in the details
and didn't recognize what he
read.)

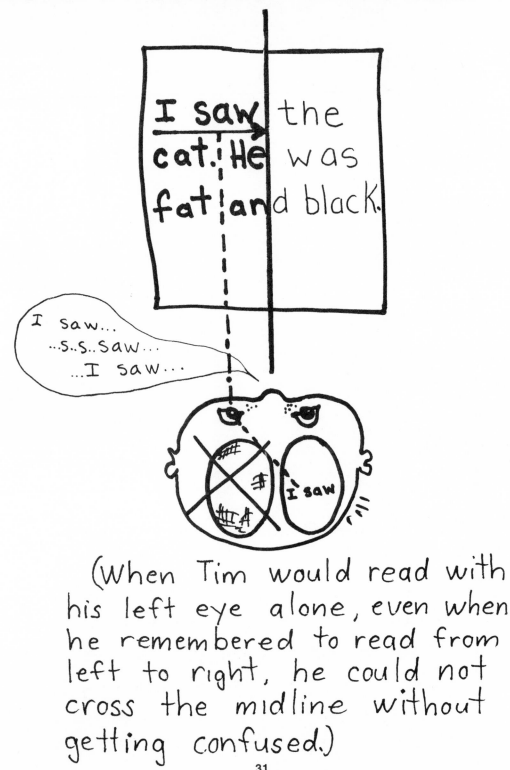

(When Tim would read with his left eye alone, even when he remembered to read from left to right, he could not cross the midline without getting confused.)

what's it about?
Hmm.... A mouse.

Sadly he slipped the last crumbs of his peanut butter sandwich into the knothole. "If you're in there, Herman, I'm ready to be friends again." There was no answer, but the breadcrumbs disappeared...

Mouse At School!

(Tim can "sight read" with his language "try" brain switched off. He may "sound" good in the classroom reading circle. However, Tim never remembers what he has read).

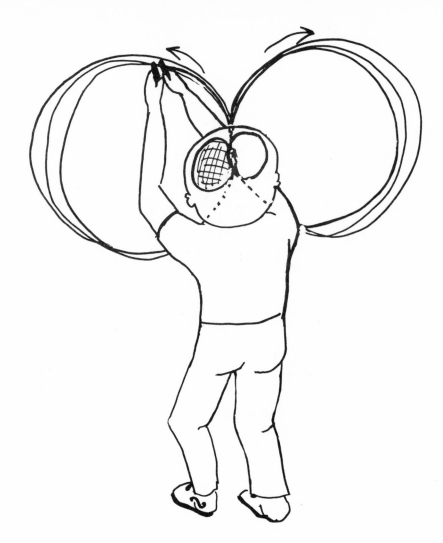

(The lazy 8, drawn first with each hand separately, then with both hands together, switches on both brains simultaneously. Tracking exercises no longer switch off and are beneficial!)

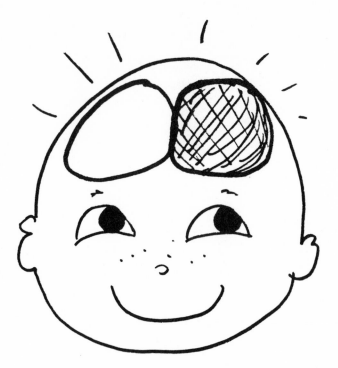

I check strong now reading
with both eyes!

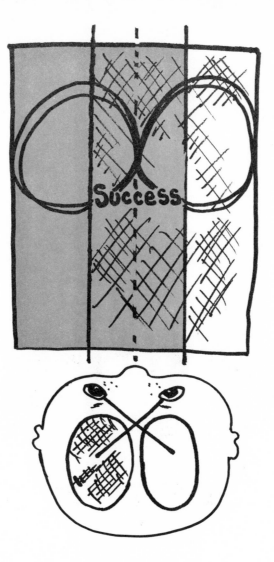

When I learned to use both brain hemispheres at one time, the <u>midline</u> began to disappear and I could work in the <u>midfield</u> with both eyes for integrated learning!

Writing and Lazy 8's

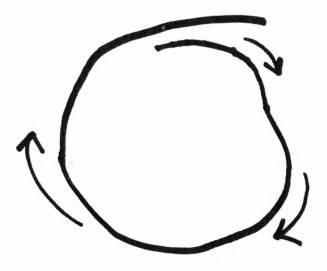

Before I learned to cross the midline for writing, I made my circles backwards (clockwise, not counterclockwise).

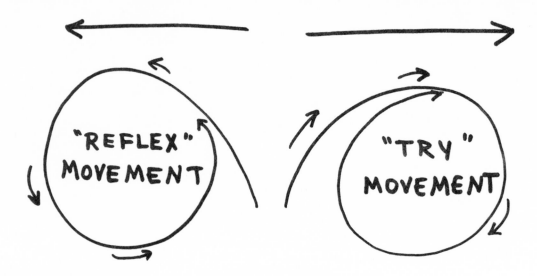

Movement which originates in the language "try" brain flows from the midline toward the right. Movement which originates in the "reflex" brain flows from the midline toward the left. When both brains are "on" together, movement can flow either way.

(When Tim wrote with the "reflex" brain switched off and the "try" brain on alone, he formed all his letters on the right side of the midline. He could never feel any difference between "b" and "d". The tricks he learned to tell the difference never worked.)

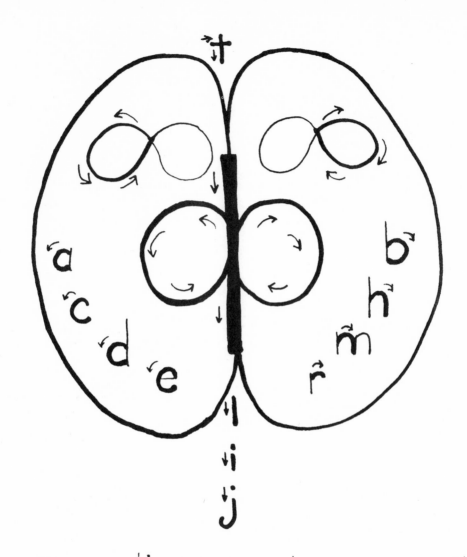

I practiced my lazy 8's with Eddy until I could write with both hemispheres "switched on". The "b" and "d" feel totally different now, and I can write automatically, without trying!

Crossing the Midline for Listening and Memory

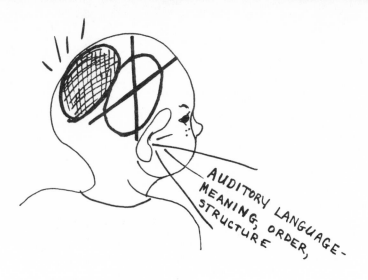

AUDITORY LANGUAGE-
MEANING, ORDER,
STRUCTURE

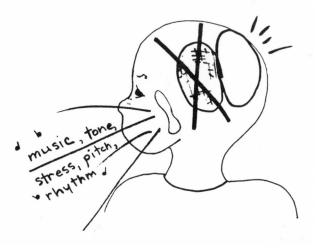

music, tone,
stress, pitch,
rhythm

Eddie said that when I turn my head to the right I am listening with my language brain ear. When I turn my head to the left, I use my "musical" ear that doesn't care much about language.

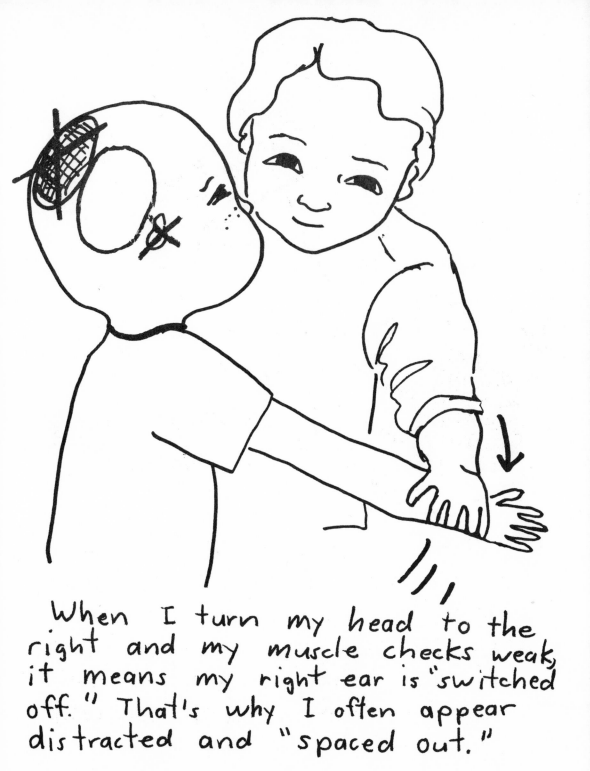

When I turn my head to the right and my muscle checks weak, it means my right ear is "switched off." That's why I often appear distracted and "spaced out."

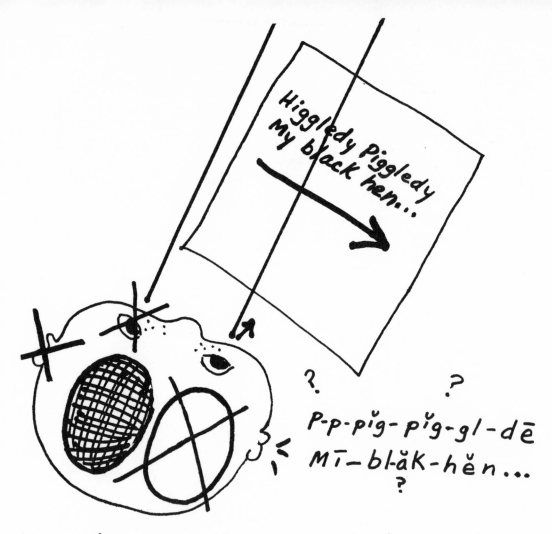

(Tim is listening to his voice decode the story with his language "try" ear alone. He may not be able to remember what he has read, nor will he be able to read it with expression or feeling.)

(Tim may be listening to the sounds of the words and he may be visualizing some images. Without the language "try" brain on, he may appear to be daydreaming and will not be able to answer questions.)

45

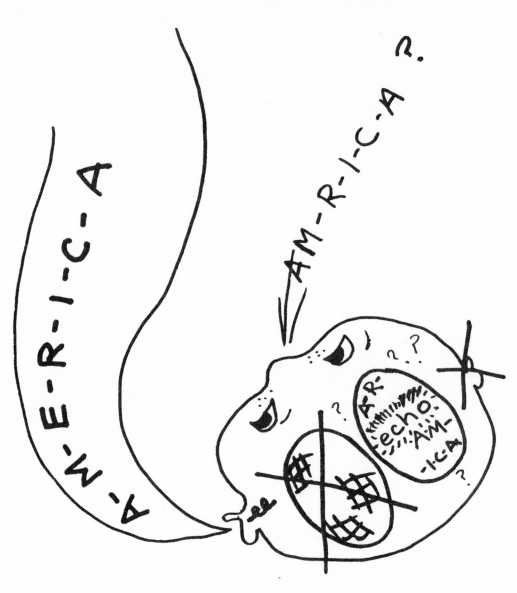

(Tim is learning to spell by "reflex" clues alone. He needs the meaning, logic, and order of the language "try" brain.)

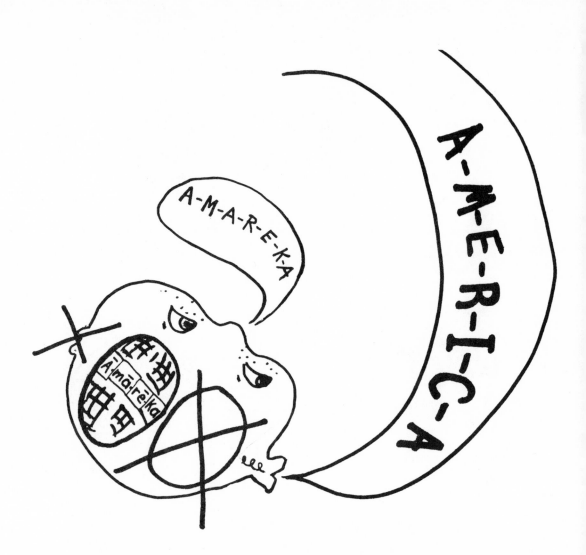

(Tim is learning to spell by the rules preferred by the language "try" brain without hearing the rhythm and music of the vowels, perceived only by the "reflex" brain.)

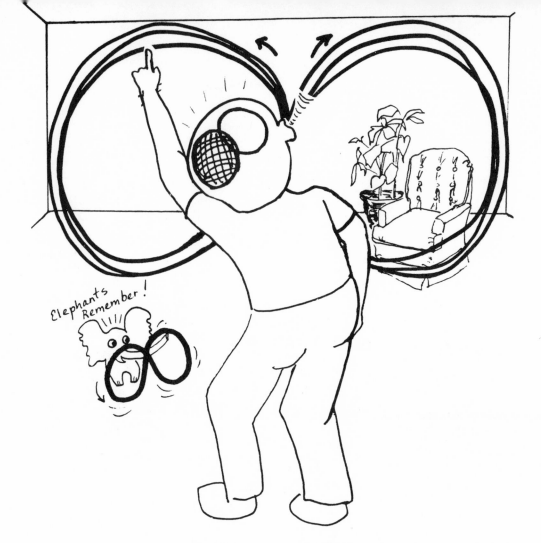

Elephants Remember!

I learned to "switch on" thinking with both my ears by doing "The Elephant." I trace a lazy 8 with each arm while holding my shoulder against my ear. My whole upper body moves as a solid unit as I focus beyond my hand.

Crossing the Midline for Stress

(Tim is stressed by "trying too hard" and cannot remember and use his imagination. He has too much energy in the "try" brain.)

(Whenever Tim feels that he
is "trying" yet not thinking
with his whole brain, he holds
his forehead on two points
between his eyes and his hairline. This "switches on" his
"reflex" brain again. He calls
these spots his "positive
points.")

(Tim sometimes cannot settle
down and get started with
all he wants to do. He is
"reversed" by overstimulation
and has too much energy in
the "reflex" brain.)

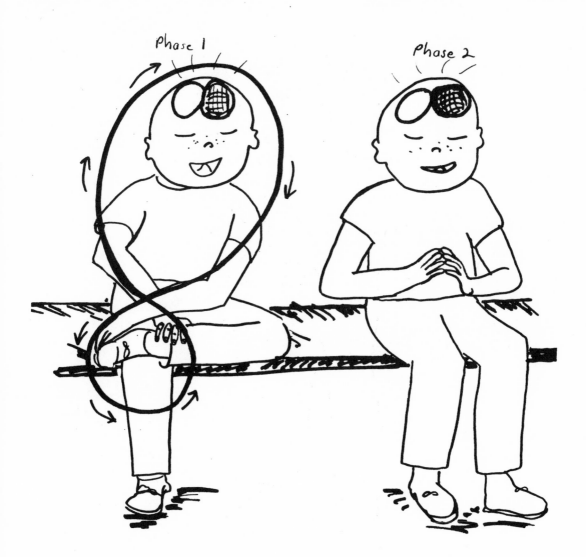

I do my Cook's Hook-ups
whenever I cannot concentrate
and need more energy in my
"try" brain.

Before reading a book, I rub my "brain buttons" (two points just below the collarbone to the right and left of the sternum) while placing my hand over my navel.

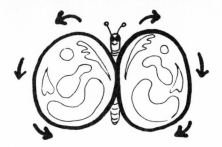

I imagine a butterfly on the ceiling and I trace its wings with my nose. This helps me to focus better. To make my neck stronger, I grasp my neck at the sides or the back while I trace the wings.

I put on my "thinking cap"
before listening or speaking
by rubbing my ears, from
inside out and from top to
bottom. This helps me to
listen, pay attention and
remember.

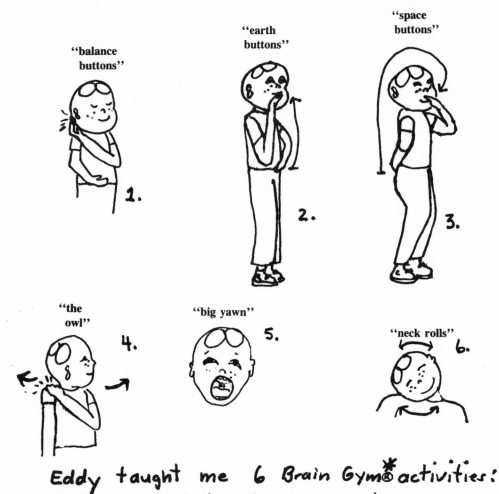

"balance buttons"

"earth buttons"

"space buttons"

1.

2.

3.

"the owl"

4.

"big yawn"

5.

"neck rolls"

6.

Eddy taught me 6 Brain Gym* activities:
1. For balance, I hold the bone behind my ear while touching my navel.
2. For receptive energy, I hold below my lips and in front of my pubic bone.
3. For expressive energy, I hold above my lips and my tailbone at the same time.
4. To relax, I squeeze my shoulders, one at a time, while turning my head slowly each way.
5 To relax my jaw and eyes, I yawn big and loud
6. To cross the midline, I do neck rolls, s-l-o-w-l-y.
* See <u>Brain Gym</u>,® Dennison and Dennison, 1986.

I do the Skip-a-Cross
everyday. This is like the
cross crawl, done to music,
with a hop and a skip.

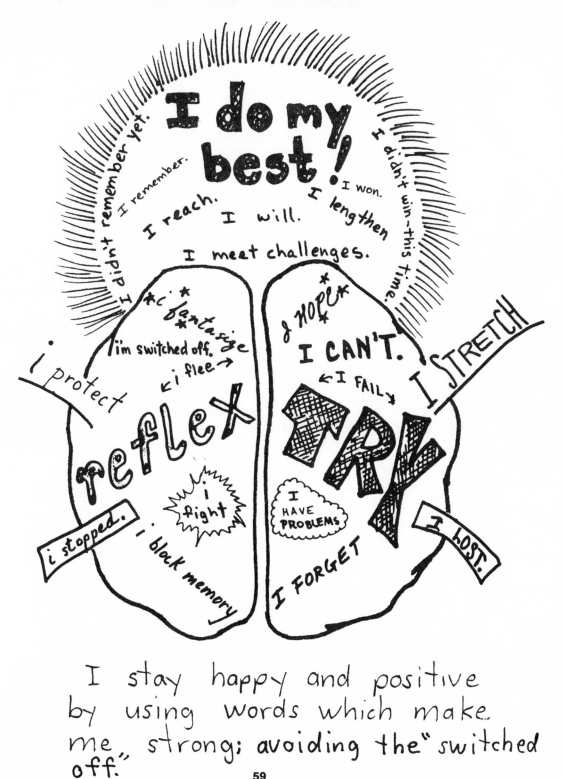

I do my best!

I didn't remember yet.
I remember.
I reach.
I will.
I won.
I lengthen
I didn't win—this time.
I meet challenges.

c fantasize
i'm switched off.
←i flee→
I HOPE
I CAN'T.
←I FAIL→
I STRETCH

i protect
reflex
TRY

i stopped.
i fight
I HAVE PROBLEMS
i black memory
I FORGET
I LOST.

I stay happy and positive
by using words which make
me strong; avoiding the "switched
off."

CHILD'S ONE-SIDED (SWITCHED-OFF) PERSPECTIVES

1. No matter how hard I try, I am always failing. I must be hopeless.

2. I am clumsy and often hurt myself, no matter how I try to be careful.

3. I often feel lost around other children, but I can do better for an adult who will praise (or scold) me.

4. I want to be better than the other kids (the toughest, fastest, cutest, smartest, or meanest), no matter what!

5. No one seems to understand my meaning when I read and sometimes I even get confused when I talk. As for writing, it is just to please the teacher. What could the purpose be?

CHILD'S INTEGRATED PERSPECTIVES

1. I do my best at whatever I do, happily exploring possibilities. I never feel like "giving up."

2. I enjoy moving! I am happy climbing, running, and exploring my physical abilities.

3. I set my own goals and I feel good about achieving them, no matter what others might think.

4. I enjoy improving upon whatever I do, each time I do it. I respect others for their unique learning styles.

5. I like to write my own stories, and my ideas and thoughts seem to flow out onto the paper. When I read, I always seem to know what will happen next. When I talk, the words come out and immediately make sense to me as soon as I feel the thought.

PARENT/TEACHER'S ONE-SIDED PERSPECTIVE

1. No matter how hard I try, my child (student) fails to learn. He must be hopeless.

2. My child (class) has a life of its own, over which I have no control. This energy sometimes overwhelms me, as if I have no conscious choice about what happens.

3. I praise or scold my child (student) so that he will always seek to work up to *my* standards.

4. I never let the children see my weaknesses and failings. Adults should be role models for children and children must learn that the parent (teacher) is the ultimate authority.

5. I try my hardest to communicate, but my child (student) often seems confused. I know I must keep teaching (parenting) though, as he is incapable of learning on his own.

PARENT/TEACHER'S INTEGRATED PERSPECTIVES

1. I give my child (student) tasks in which he can succeed, so he experiences many "wins" every day, and is not afraid of new challenges!

2. I enjoy my child's (student's) high energy. I seem to anticipate events so that I feel I am making the right choices and am challenged to guide overall situations when the stress level is intense.

3. I guide my child (student) to discover the work *he* loves and to experience the intrinsic reward of personal achievement.

4. I allow myself to be vulnerable and a real person in front of my child (student), teaching him that even adults continue to learn and to grow. I expect that my child (student) will use my learning as a step to his own growth, and that he will become even greater than myself.

5. I love to parent (teach) and learn so much from my child (student)! My relationship with him keeps my ideas flowing. My daily life takes on renewed meaning as it is transformed through the magic of human exchange.

REFERENCE FOR PARENTS AND EDUCATORS
WHY WE BELIEVE IN MUSCLE CHECKING

Within the first few years of life, the child, full of a dynamic energy difficult for most adults to imitate, makes tremendous leaps in learning. The receptive brain allows the child to recognize and reproduce the speech sounds around him and turns this information into self-generating language! This feat is done by most human beings *without conscious thought.* By age 5, however, many of us are already stuck in a pattern of learning which requires repetition and drill, without the previous zest for discovery, as if nothing new could be as intrinsically rewarding as exploring how to crawl, walk, run, and speak as a pre-school child.

How can we retrieve that natural, joyful love of learning? Thousands of students have rediscovered, in Educational Kinesiology, their innate ability to learn. In Brain Gym® we believe a switched-on muscle is one of the best intrinsic rewards anyone can experience! The purpose of this book is to guide you, the Basic Brain Gym® student, parent, or teacher, to begin to work with Educational Kinesiology in way that has immediate results for you and the student.

The strong muscle is our way of listening to the body's highest intuitive wisdom about its own natural process of neurological growth. We never second guess the muscle check! When the student "learns" more useful neurological patterns and "unlearns" those patterns adopted because of physical or emotional trauma, or through efforts to mold himself to the patterns of others. his innate, most healthy pattern of growth is able to unfold!

The best teacher will "anchor" his student with success after success—never pushing the child beyond the limits of what he has the ability to achieve. A wise teacher, using Educational Kinesiology in his teaching, will anchor positive movement and response with encouraging words, actions, and a "switched on" muscle check.

WHY DOES EDUCATIONAL KINESIOLOGY WORK?

Cross-crawling, or patterning, has been recognized for years as a technique to restore neurological functioning when there has been severe brain damage. It has proven effective in vision training as practiced by developmental optometrists as well. During the 1960's, Drs. Doman and Delacato announced that, in addition to reversing brain damage, children in their patterning program could also learn to read better. Creeping and crawling instantly became popular at many schools across the nation. Unfortunately, educators could not replicate these findings with children in the classroom, and movement experiences were relegated once again to the P.E. departments.

CRAWLING ALONE PROVES NOT ENOUGH!

Cross-crawling has obviously helped many people and disappointed countless others as well. Crawling *should* be the most perfect brain balance exercise, and, theoretically it is. Since it requires both cerebral hemispheres to be activated to complete the crawling step, each brain operating the opposite side of the body, the more one crawls, the better integrated and balanced he should become!

However, the human nervous system is not quite so simplistic. Educational Kinesiology has the unique ability to study the relationship of movement and brain function through the use of muscle checking, making it possible to explain why cross-crawling has helped some people and not others, and why crawling in the classroom has proven unreliable as an educational tool. Further, our research into cross-crawl has resulted in a correction procedure: **Dennison Laterality Repatterning.** When this procedure is practiced, as taught in Brain Gym® workshops, it makes cross-crawl and all bilateral activities the effective tools they should be in balancing the brain for improved academic performance, as well as for physical, mental, and spiritual health!

REFLEX DOMINANCE FOR BI-LATERAL MOVEMENT

Crawling seems only to be of therapeutic benefit to those who learn it thoroughly, in infancy, before the "left" or "try brain" develops its sense of conscious awareness. When people who crept and crawled as babies cross-crawl they test "right" or "reflex brain" dominant for the movement of their bodies, freeing their "left brains" to learn new things. When people learn to crawl later in life, they tend to be too self-conscious of their bodies and test "left brain" dominant for the movement, unable to access the "right brain" to take over this action once it is mastered.

HOMOLATERAL OR INTEGRATED PATTERNS

When a person checks "right brain" activated for crawling his indicator muscle response is "switched on," suggesting that hemispheric integration is taking place. When a person checks "left brain" activated his indicator muscle response is "switched off," indicating that hemispheric integration is failing to take place and that his energy is being diminished. We call the former people "bi-lateral," or "laterally integrated," indicating that both sides are operative, and the latter people "homolateral," indicating that *only one brain is on at a time.* All those people who would have checked left-brained and "off" with an indicator muscle when cross-crawling would not have benefitted from crawling in the classroom or patterning for dyslexia as it has been traditionally prescribed! It is our experience, with the population identified as "learning disabled" that 80% or more will fall into the "homolateral" category. *Educational Kinesiology For Kids* can help this group to join the "laterally integrated" population which is able to learn with the whole brain more easily.

BRAIN/BODY COOPERATION—
"SWITCHED ON" ON "SWITCHED OFF"?

The right brain hemisphere controls the left side of the body and the consciousness of the left eye and ear. Likewise, the left brain hemisphere is in charge of the right side of the body and the right eye and ear. The nerves to the muscles and sense organs cross over from the opposite controlling brain hemisphere. When one side of the brain is active, the other side may do one of two things; it may cooperate and coordinate its movements with the controlling hemisphere, or it may "switch off" and block integration.

The "laterally integrated" person is someone who has learned how to use both his brain hemispheres as a whole system; the homolateral or "switched off" person is someone who has yet to use more than one small part of his abilities at a given time. Our early childhood experiences determine how our brain develops. Unfortunately, when we are successful at a "switched off" behavior—one that is a compensation for a stress or trauma, we tend to repeat it over and over again, blocking further learning. Likewise, if we achieve success at a neurologically organized behavior, that experience becomes a springboard for further learning and growth!

OUR INTERNAL "MIDLINE" - THE CORPUS CALLOSUM

In order for the right and left brain to work in integrated fashion, the two brain hemispheres are interconnected by the corpus callosum, an intricate bundle of nerve fibers. Ideally, in infancy, this complex system of switches develops as we first creep and crawl to synchronize and integrate information so that the two hemispheres can work together through life in harmony and coordination. One hemisphere can take over for the other and can also operate on its own side to process a given task. To learn a new task easily, *both* sides of the brain need to be involved in the operation through continual communication across this midline!

WHY WE NEED BOTH BRAINS

We need both brain hemispheres because each brain perceives reality in totally and uniquely different ways! The "right" brain (identified in this text as the "reflex" brain) is capable of grouping the biggest picture or "whole" available. For example, it enables us to recognize a face in a crowd or to know a song after hearing only one or two notes. The "left" brain (identified in this text as the "try" brain) is logical, orderly and verbal. It enables us to break things up into small bits of information in computer-like fashion, so that we can learn new things, one at a time, and communicate with each other. Neither brain was meant to ever work alone, by itself. Both brains working together enable learning to be fun and effortless.

THE REFLEX/GESTALT BRAIN

The "right" hemisphere, when working alone, is little more than a "reflex" brain. It receives information through the senses; however, it is unable to express itself or to use the data creatively. The gestalting abilities to intuit and to know, to make associations and to remember, require cooperation with the left brain. The more one achieves integration in life, through Brain Gym® or other processes, the more the "right" brain can work at its best and the less it needs to work by "reflex" or instinct!

THE TRY/ANALYTIC BRAIN

The "left" brain, when working alone, is little more than a "try brain." It is critical judgmental, and analytical. Without the gestalt sense, it cannot remember what it learns and must do things over and over. When working with the gestalt brain, through Edu-Kinesthetics integration, the "left" brain is the expressive brain where learning is internalized and made a part of the Self. It is through movement expression that one knows that he has learned and prepares for the next step in growth and awareness!

THE BRAIN GYM® WORKSHOPS

The BRAIN GYM® WORKSHOPS help adult participants to experience more and better integrated learning, performance and daily living. Techniques utilizing the modern science of Edu-Kinesthetics muscle checking will be taught. These tools enable students to guide others to heightened integration as well. The importance of movement across the "midline" is the focus of this class which is designed to correct homolaterality or lack of analytic/gestalt brain integration.

"Integration" is a continual, lifelong process. Continual growth throughout the life of the individual depends upon successful completion of basic developmental skills such as creeping, crawling, skipping, reading, writing, and so forth, as taught in this class. Further development of the individual is then available through the Edu-Kinesthetics Advanced Seminar.

SWITCHING OFF ON THE MIDLINE

In order to read fluently, to write creatively, to spell and remember, to listen and think at the same time, we must be able to "cross the midline" which connects the right and the left brain. Though we all cross it to some extent, this midline is still a bridge or a barrier for learning depending upon our prior learning experiences. When right and left brain communicate spontaneously, working together at one time, then the midline becomes a bridge, connecting neurological pathways. When right and left brain must take turns working, then the midline becomes a barrier and the connection is broken.

THE MIDLINE

LEFT FIELD	MIDFIELD	RIGHT FIELD
RIGHT BRAIN LEARNING	INTEGRATED LEARNING	LEFT BRAIN LEARNING
	MIDLINE ➡	

People may have a midline barrier for many reasons which are taught in the BRAIN GYM® WORKSHOPS. Usually the cause is homolaterality, either in the life energy as a whole, or in the energy systems affecting the eyes, ears, or body coordination. The homolateral person is limited to "one-sided" thinking because he has access to only one side of the brain at a time. He must "switch off" one side each time he wants to use the other, in alternating fashion. The homolateral person always experiences a coordination problem at some level, depending upon the severity of his disability. Whether it affects his eyes, his ears, his body as a whole, or one of the countless other ways he might "switch off," he must learn to "cross the midline" before his behavior can change.

Many examples of "switching off on the midline" are included in this book. If a child "switches off" the analytic "try brain" ear in school, he may become so absorbed in the gestalt sense, (such as the tone of the teacher's voice or outside noises), that he pays no attention to the meaning of words and be labelled a "daydreamer" or "hyperactive." As a reader he might "switch off" his gestalt "reflex" eye, therefore able to break words down into sounds but unable to blend them back into whole units and to store them into his long-term visual memory. The possible combinations of "switching off" are as endless and unique as the possibilities for creative potential as we become more integrated!

USING EDUCATIONAL KINESIOLOGY, STEP-BY-STEP
THE ART OF BASIC MUSCLE CHECKING

1. You the teacher and your student begin with a few seconds of massage of Brain Buttons while holding the navel. Then do a minute of Cook's Hook-ups, while breathing deeply. This will prepare you to get the best results with your muscle checks (see pages 5 and 6).

2. Use common sense about muscle checking. Ask if there is a reason (injury or other) why you shouldn't push on your student's arm.

3. Tell your student to hold his arm out straight.

4. Tell him you are going to push on his arm and for him to do his best to stay strong and hold the arm up. Give a clue like "hold," or have him say "push," then check. If you both agree this is strong, then proceed!

5. This locked muscle is what you both are looking for! (Simple so far?) Let your student experience this strength by modifying your pressure to meet his. Your pressure is light, but sustained as you "lean" into the check. Never push so hard that either of you experience strain or needless effort. You have now both experienced a strong muscle! If the student cannot easily "hold" with a strong muscle—**stop.** Find a Brain Gym instructor who can help you.

6. Play with muscle checking! It's fun. Ask your student to "try harder." Notice that the harder he "tries" the easier it is to push the arm down. Ask your student to "do his best." Re-check and see how much stronger he is. Explain that it is "OK" to be "switched off" when he tries. Go back and forth between "try" and "do your best" until you both can tell which is "switched on" and which is "switched off." (When you are "brain checking," the "switched on" muscle lets you know that there is no inhibition of energy from the motor centers of the brain to the muscle—so the reflex brain, or both brains, are "switched on." The "switched off" muscle tells you there is conscious thought **alone**—the "try" or "left" brain by itself—and exertion is necessary to hold the arm up. Explain to your student that it is **good** to be "switched off" on conscious control, as this means he can really concentrate when he needs to. Conscious control should be the "low gear," so it is never as strong as automatic control and **neither** are as solid as the "high gear" of integrated strength!)

7. Savor with your student the pleasurable experience of strength when his body works easily and automatically!

DENNISON LATERALITY REPATTERNING

Before commencing this repatterning procedure, you and your student do the Brain Buttons exercise and the Cook's Hook-Ups as shown on pages 5 and 6.

1. **CHECKING** (Movement Biofeedback)

   A. Check a strong indicator muscle in the clear.

   B. Have the student cross-crawl, touching hand to opposite knee, for 10-20 repetitions. Each side once is a full repetition.

   C. Check the indicator muscle. Note: Is it on or off? If it is off, the student may be homolateral. Confirm the finding with the remaining checks.

   D. Have the student homolateral crawl, touching hand to the same knee, for 10-20 repetitions.

   E. Check the indicator muscle. Note: Is it on or off? If it is on, the student is homolateral and needs repatterning.

   F. Have student look at an **X**. If **X** switches off the indicator muscle, the student is homolateral.

   G. Have student look at two parallel vertical lines, **II**. If this switches on the indicator muscle, the student is homolateral.

2. **REPATTERNING** (Pages 11 through 26)

   A. Muscle check the student to see if he/she is ready for further integration. If so, proceed. If not, wait for a more appropriate time.

   B. Have the student cross-crawl, as in number 1A above, with eyes purposefully turned to access the reflex brain. This is usually up to the left, as reflex is on the right side of the brain for most people.

   C. Re-check the indicator muscle, noting that it is now on for cross-crawl, not off. If it is still off, have your student cross-crawl with his eyes up to the right. Repeat the muscle check. The brain should now be "on."

   D. Have the student homolateral crawl, as in number 1D above, with eyes turned to access the analytic brain. This would be down to the right if 2B was eyes up left, indicating that the analytic brain is on the left side.

   E. Re-check the indicator muscle, noting that it is now off for this activity (not strong). If it is not off, do more repetitions, or continue with eyes down to the left, instead of the right.

3. INTEGRATION

A. Have the student slowly clasp his/her two hands together to symbolically integrate the two brain hemispheres, "feeling the two brains working together."

B. Have the student cross-crawl with eyes looking in all directions.

C. Re-check the indicator muscle. It should be "on," no matter where the student directs his/her eyes.

D. Have the student homolateral crawl with eyes looking in all directions.

E. Re-check the indicator muscle. It should be "off," no matter where the student directs his/her eyes.

F. Re-check looking at the **X.** The indicator muscle should now be "on."

G. Re-check looking at the **II.** The indicator muscle should now be "off."

H. Discuss the changes the student is experiencing. This has been a moment of rebirth for thousands of people!

Dennison Laterality Repatterning is effective because it works in accord with *Nature* as she intended us to learn. This patterning gives people permission to cross the midline, restoring the natural process of the infant to trust, to let go of conscious control, and to access the right-brain for movement. **Dennison Laterality Repatterning** seems simple, yet requires instruction to go from step to step. If you have not experienced it yet, ask a Brain Gym® instructor to repattern you. If you know the technique, repattern as many people as you can!

Dennison Laterality Repatterning is not suggested as a panacea for all our ills. As a part of any sound educational or health maintenance program, it very often provides results for people who have failed to find help elsewhere. It is literally true, as many are learning, that we must crawl before we walk.

CROSSING THE MIDLINE FOR READING

In order to determine if the midline is blocked in terms of vision:

1. Check a strong indicator muscle in the clear.

2. Have the student read, or have him imagine he is reading, and re-check the muscle. If it is "off," go to #3.

3. Check the person looking at a target (a pencil or penlight) in the right visual field. Then check the person looking at the target in the left visual field. Now back again to the right visual field. If the person cannot switch from one field to the other, easily, then he is "switched off" at the visual level. This "switching off" may affect both eyes or only one eye. Since vision is so involved in most human activity, people who are "switched off" are usually "switched" at the visual level (see page 30).

4. If the person checks "on" for #3 above, check the person to see if reading for one-half hour would cause "switching off." This is done by asking the student to follow a target back and forth across the midline for twenty repetitions. This is called tracking. If this activity induces "switching off" then reading or eye exercises would have a negative impact.

5. To repattern, determine if the student will check "switched on" while you say, "This system is ready to achieve further integration for reading." If yes, the student would do the "Lazy 8" exercise for the eyes.

CROSSING THE MIDLINE FOR WRITING

1. Check a strong indicator in the clear.

2. Check the person on the alphabet, thinking about it as a whole and, if "switched off," on specific letters.

3. Check the person while thinking about writing or on reading what he has written.

4. If the person checks "off" on #2 and #3 above, then he has not learned to cross the midline for writing and he is still using his language brain to form letters when it should be free to express ideas. This can happen only when the movement for writing comes automatically from the gestalt (reflex) brain. To correct this learning blockage, the student does the lazy 8 for writing with you (also, see page 40).

CROSSING THE MIDLINE FOR LISTENING AND MEMORY

1. Check a strong indicator muscle in the clear.

2. Check the person on digit spans or oral spelling up to the limits of his memory. Then re-check the indicator muscle. Did the experience "switch him off?"

3. Muscle check the person with his head turned all the way to the left, and again with the head turned all the way to the right. Do either of these positions result in "switching off" as well?

4. If either test in #3 above produces a "switched off" response, the person listens, both externally and internally, with only one ear at a time. He must "switch off" one ear in order to use the other. This is how he has learned to listen! If the proprioception (sense of movement) between the brain and the neck muscles is comfortable while turning to the right (activating the left brain) then the right ear is "switched on." If, however, turning to the right "switches him off," then the connection between brain, neck, and ear is not familiar and comfortable, and the right ear will not be used with the left when listening and thinking. To repattern, the student does the Lazy 8 for memory, an exercise called "The Elephant" (see page 48).

THE LAZY 8

The Lazy 8, or infinity sign, has been used in special education and vision training for many years because it usually gets results. The Lazy 8 has been validated by Brain Gym® muscle checking. It works successfully because it enables the student to cross the midline with a continuous line, thus preventing him from switching off his right brain energy flow. The Lazy 8 is a symbol which "centers" people temporarily, thus opening the nervous system to more energy while its effects last. The effect is to temporarily balance the brain hemispheres so that the integrated learning can be experienced and stored.

Several innovations in using the Lazy 8 have been developed out of our Educational Kinesiology research. These techniques make the Lazy 8 that much more effective. We have found that these exercises need only be done once, correctly, to act as a permanent repatterning for specific tasks! Daily reinforcement is a joyful reminder of new potential.

LAZY 8'S FOR VISION AND READING

The teacher draws a Lazy 8 on the chalkboard. It should be as large as the student can reach comfortably with either arm while standing at the midline or center.

The student traces the Lazy 8, always moving up at the midline, counterclockwise to the left, clockwise to the right. The student traces the Lazy 8 first with one hand, then with the other, and then with both hands moving together (in the same direction). Three traces each time is sufficient, then muscle check to see if both hemispheres are on, and if "switching off" of the eyes is corrected. Tracking to strengthen eye muscle coordination and hand-eye coordination exercises should only be done after the Lazy 8 exercise has been completed and the student knows he is staying "switched on" by the anchoring of the strong muscle check!

LAZY 8'S FOR WRITING

In order to print, and to later write in cursive script, the energy from the movement centers of the brain must flow as one forms, first lines into letters, and then, letters into words. The lower case letters are formed by integrating the "counterclockwise" and "clockwise" circles of the Lazy 8 with a vertical line at the center. When the student can feel the Lazy 8 as he writes each letter, writing becomes easier and more automatic, and writing problems begin to disappear (see page 40).

LAZY 8 FOR MEMORY (MATH, SPELLING)

The student draws the Lazy 8 against a fixed plane on the horizon (see page 48) with an imaginary paintbrush extended from his outstretched arm. The head and shoulders are locked so that the whole body draws the figure with no separate movement of the head, neck, and shoulders. Make sure the knees bend and that the body sways rhythmically from side to side. This acts to switch on the proprioception in the neck related to listening, speaking, and memory.

In Educational Kinesiology we recognize that all learning is task specific. In human behavior we cannot depend upon "transfer" from one learning experience to another, even if a "logical" relationship may be apparent. As the teacher develops a relationship with the student, she should help him do Lazy 8's on all subjects, and aspects of subjects, which may need better integration. When used after Dennison Laterality Repatterning, and with the other Brain Gym® activities, as taught in **Educational Kinesiology (Edu-K) for Kids**, the Lazy 8 is a tool to permanently integrate those activities which had, beforehand, been done in a "switched off," or homolateral, manner.

BRAIN GYM® WITH A GROUP

DENNISON LATERALITY REPATTERNING

Class sessions should begin with a drink of water for everybody, the "brain buttons" exercise, and "Cook's Hook-Ups." Notice the pleasant change in the room as everyone begins to feel more centered, grounded, and aware.

CHECKING

1. Have 4 or 5 students cross crawl in place. Check each one. "Off" or "on?"

2. Next, have the students look at an **X**. Those "switched on" for cross crawl are usually "on" for **X**. Those "switched off" for cross crawl are, likewise, usually "off" for **X**.

3. Next, have these students homolateral crawl and re-check. Most students who need repatterning are "off" for this movement.

4. Have these students look at **II**. People who are "on" for homolateral crawl are usually "on" for **II**.

REPATTERNING

5. Anyone who is not "on" for cross crawl and **X** and not "off" for homolateral crawl and **II** could benefit from repatterning!

6. Have students cross crawl, eyes directed up to the left. Help those who get confused and cannot seem to stop doing the homolateral crawl. Re-check after 8-10 repetitions, or when the movement seems fun and automatic. They should now check "switched on." The body/mind system learns quickly when a better and easier way of moving is offered. Anyone who does not check "on" should stand aside for a moment, while you complete the repatterning with those who did.

7. Now have them do a homolateral crawl, with eyes directed down to the right. After 8-10 repetitions, they should check "off."

8. Anchor that the students need no longer point eyes up/down to test "on"/"off" for these movements by having them cross crawl while looking in all directions. Muscle check "on." Homolateral crawl while looking in all directions. Muscle check "off."

9. Have them slowly bring their hands together, interlocking the fingers, and feel the two brains working together better, as one.

10. Those who did not check "switched on" in #6 above should be repatterned on cross crawl with eyes up to the right, instead of to the left (check as "on") and homolateral crawl with eyes down to the left (check as "off").

11. Once your entire group is repatterned, this process need not ever be repeated. In subsequent sessions, the whole group will benefit from all bilateral movements, i.e., walking, running, climbing, etc., and, cross crawl and skip-a-cross will be beneficial additions to your daily program.

BRAIN GYM REPATTERNING OF BEHAVIOR

In Educational Kinesiology we believe that all behavior, both positive and negative, is caused by movement, or lack of movement due to blockages in the neurological wiring of the individual. We believe there are no bad, naughty, lazy, aggressive, sloppy. . . children. We believe these "behaviors" can be corrected in the group situation, through Dennison Laterality Repatterning (above) and through use of the "Positive Points" and "Cook's Hook-Ups" as shown in this book.

THE POSITIVE POINTS

The "Positive Points" are neuro-vascular holding points on the frontal eminences found half-way between the eyebrows and the hairline. When lightly held, by oneself or another, these points are helpful to repattern conditioned responses to emotionally charged thoughts about people, places, memories, tasks, and environmental factors.

1. Check the student to find a strong muscle which you cannot weaken easily. Talk about it to the class and keep it fun.

2. Have the student think quietly about a school subject, classmate, or anything that makes him uncomfortable.

3. Re-check the strong muscle. It will now be "switched off" if stress is present.

4. Hold the student's "Positive Points" lightly (usually for 20-30 seconds) with just enough pressure to pull the skin taut between the two points, while instructing the student to think of the same thing (school book, friend's face, etc.) which led him to "switch off."

5. Re-check the muscle. The muscle will now be "switched on" if the process is complete. Some stressful issues require holding the points for a longer period of time. Discuss with the student how he feels about the issue now. Is there a change? Observe behavior in the future. Hold class discussions about behavior and how to change it.

6. Teach the class how to find and hold the "Positive Points."

COOK'S HOOK-UPS

Cook's Hook-Ups are "postures" which realign the energy of the body when it is disturbed by forces beyond the conscious control of the individual such as weather, processed foods, magnetic fields, etc. Children, whatever their socio-economic group, come to school having experienced stress from these forces. Television, computers, automobiles, family conflicts, poor diet, the anapestic beat of certain rock music, etc., can overstimulate a child and leave him unable to adjust to the classroom environment. A wonderful way to make the transition from the uncontrollable outside world to the peaceful, secure place of learning is Cook's Hook-Ups.

Students, individually or in a circle, can do Cook's Hook-Ups together as depicted on page 6.

1. Student places the left ankle over the right knee.
2. Student hooks-up his right hand to his left ankle.
3. Student hooks-up his left palm to his left foot (over the ball).
4. Student holds this position for one minute, breathing deeply, with eyes closed; tongue may be placed against the roof of the mouth during inhale.
5. Next, student uncrosses legs and places the fingertips together while continuing to breathe deeply for one minute.

Teachers who use this technique often include it as part of a sharing circle, either passing a heart or a peacepipe. Students are given the opportunity to speak out on whatever is on their minds.

Cook's Hook-Ups help students to focus their attention on the classroom and to leave the stresses of the outside world behind them.

Students should do Cook's Hook-Ups whenever they feel anxious, afraid or angry, or seem unable to concentrate.

DEFINITION OF TERMS

ANALYTIC — Refers to the ability to perceive reality as isolated, separate parts without attention to their context as a whole.

BLENDING — The synthesis of separate parts, such as phonetic speech sounds, into longer, more meaningful, wholes.

COMPENSATORY APPROACH — The approach to education for learning disabilities which emphasizes that children must accept their situation and learn to adjust to it by maximizing a strength and compensating for any weaknesses.

CROSS DOMINANCE — The inherited predisposition to be dominant with one hand, usually the right, and dominant with the alternate eye and/or ear at the same time.

DECODE — The analysis of any symbolic language into a meaningful message.

DOMINANCE — The inherited preference for one cerebral hemisphere over the other for handedness, eyedness, earedness, etc.

DYSLEXIA — The inability to decode the printed symbol due to the inhibition of the receptive centers of the brain. Broadly, any learning disability which causes confusion and requires compensatory behaviors.

ECHO-EFFECT — The memory of the spoken symbol by sound alone, without attention to meaningful clues.

EDUCATIONAL KINESIOLOGY — The study of the musculature system of the body and its relationship to whole brain learning.

EDU-KINESTHETICS — The application of kinesthetics (movement) to the study of right brain, left brain, and body integration for purposes of eliminating stress and maximizing full learning potential.

ENCODE — The expression of meaning and language through the use of written symbols.

FEEDBACK — That short term memory skill which enables one to hear his own voice repeating what he has thought, read, or heard.

FEEDFORWARD — That short term memory skill which enables one to anticipate his own voice speaking something from long term memory.

GESTALT — The ability to perceive reality as a whole or totality without attention to analysis of its separate parts.

HOMOLATERAL — The involuntary choice to access only one cerebral hemisphere at any given moment, thus blocking integrated thought and movement.

IMPULSE — The intuitive response to a situation, without mediation through language or analytical thought.

INTEGRATION — The lifelong process of realizing one's physical, mental, and spiritual potential, the first step being the simultaneous activation of both cerebral hemispheres as described in this book.

MIDFIELD — The area where one visual and hemispheric field overlaps the other for integrated learning.

MIDLINE — The line which separates one visual field and hemispheric awareness from the other when there is incomplete integration.

MUSCLE CHECKING — In Edu-Kinesthetics, used for two purposes. **1.** To measure the relative strength of a muscle for the purpose of infering brain functions relevant to educators. **2.** To anchor or to reinforce positively all integrated processing.

"REFLEX" —To act without conscious thought and with self-preservation as the primary motivation. Used as a verb in Edu-Kinesthetics to suggest the movements initiated by the gestalt brain when one is homolateral and not yet integrated.

"REVERSED" — The involuntary inhibition of the language brain, due to some negativity, often resulting in movement preferred from right to left instead of from left to right, causing reading reversals.

SIMULTANEOUS PROCESSING — That ability to access both cerebral hemispheres at one and the same time, maximizing hemispheric integration and reducing stressful learning.

"SWITCHED OFF" — The involuntary inhibition of one cerebral hemisphere in order to better access the other, due to stress or lack of integration.

SYNCHRONICITY — The state of harmony in the universe where everything fits and flows together without stress. This state of consciousness begins with hemispheric integration.

"TRANSPOSED" — The inherited, neurological organization of the brain, whereby the language, speech centers are located in the right cerebral hemisphere instead of the left where they are found in 85% of the population.

ABOUT THE AUTHORS

Paul E. Dennison, Ph.D., has been an educator for all of his professional life. He is the creator of the Edu-Kinesthetics and Brain Gym processes, and a pioneer in applied brain research. His discoveries are based upon an understanding of the interdependence of physical development, language acquisition, and academic achievement. This perspective grew out of his background in curriculum development and experimental psychology at the University of Southern California, where he was granted a Doctorate in Education for his research in beginning reading achievement and its relationship to thinking. For nineteen years, Dr. Dennison served as director of the Valley Remedial Group Learning Centers in Southern California, helping children and adults turn their difficulties into successful growth. He is the author of twelve books and manuals, including *Switching On: A Guide to Edu-Kinesthetics.*

Gail E. Dennison is the co-author with her husband, Dr. Dennison, of the Edu-Kinesthetics series of books and manuals. The simple illustrations in the Edu-K books speak of her love of children and movement. As a dancer, she has brought grace and focus to the Brain Gym® activities. Gail has a varied background in the teaching of brain integration, including ten years' experience as a Touch for Health instructor. Gail's interest in perception and developmental skills comes through in the Edu-K vision courses. She developed the *Visioncircles* course and the *Vision Gym™* movements, in which rhythm, color, and form provide the basis for experiences that offer visual and perceptual growth. Gail is the creator of the *Brain Gym Journal,* and heads the publication committee for the Educational Kinesiology Foundation.

The following are some of the courses offered by the Educational Kinesiology Foundation, P.O. Box 3396, Ventura, CA 93006-3396 • (800) 356-2109

BASIC-LEVEL COURSES

★ **BRAIN GYM®** – 24 hours, consisting of Part I, **The Lateral Brain** and Part II, **The Whole Brain**
This Brain Gym course offers an in-depth experience of hemispheric integration through Dennison Laterality Repatterning and 23 Brain Gym activities that relate to whole-brain functioning. A process for achieving deeper structural integration through Three-Dimension Repatterning is also included. The effects of incomplete development of laterality, centering, and focus on posture, reading, writing, spelling, and memory are identified and balanced. Course Manual: *Brain Gym® Handbook* by Dennison and Dennison.

★ **VISIONCIRCLES** – 24 hours
The Visioncircles course provides a road map to completion of developmental skills through movement, play, and art. It offers vision enhancement through activities that nourish perceptual flexibility. Each of the eight structured sessions embodies a unique perceptual slant and emphasizes different visual and kinesthetic skills. Participants learn 34 Vision Gym movements for integrating visual, auditory, and tactile abilities. Course Manual: *The Visioncircles Handbook.* Prerequisites: Brain Gym, Parts I & II.

PROFESSIONAL-LEVEL COURSES

★ **EDU-KINESTHETICS IN DEPTH: The Seven Dimensions of Intelligence** – 32 hours
Learn and practice the Edu-Kinesthetics principles through an individualized educational model. Receive hands-on experience with seven dimensions of body movement, focusing on how each can support or block the learning process. Other areas covered in the course include: appropriate goal setting, learning theory, and growth-oriented communication. Course Manual: *Edu-Kinesthetics In Depth: The Seven Dimensions of Intelligence.* Prerequisite: Brain Gym, Parts I & II.

★ **BRAIN GYM TEACHER PRACTICUM** – 32 hours
A certification course qualifying the student to teach Brain Gym. Completion of this California state-approved course provides the graduate with specific skills for teaching the Brain Gym course. This workshop prepares the instructor to represent the Foundation in the community as a member of its staff. Course Manual: *Teacher Practicum Manual.* Prerequisite: Edu-Kinesthetics in Depth.

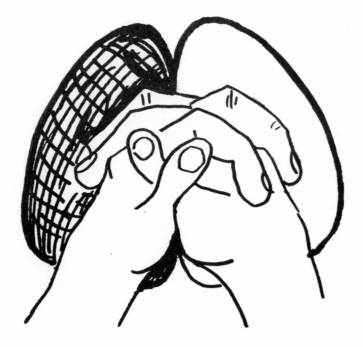

EDU-KINESTHETICS PUBLICATIONS

U.S. Funds

SWITCHING ON by Dr. Paul E. Dennison $12.95

EDU-K FOR KIDS by Dennison & Dennison $12.00

PERSONALIZED WHOLE BRAIN INTEGRATION by Dennison & Dennison $15.95

BRAIN GYM® by Dennison & Dennison .... $ 9.00

BRAIN GYM®, Teacher's Edition by Dennison & Dennison $16.95

BRAIN GYM® FOR BUSINESS by Dennison & Dennison & Teplitz .... $ 12.95

BRAIN GYM® SURFER by Hinsley & Conley .... $ 8.00

EDU-KINESTHETICS IN-DEPTH. $29.95

INTEGRATED MOVEMENTS (audio tape) $12.00

Mail your order to: **Edu-Kinesthetics, Inc.**, Post Office Box 3396, Ventura, California 93006-3396 U.S.A. Telephone or fax order with VISA/MC: Telephone (805) 650-3303 • FAX (805) 650-0524

Prices do not include postage and handling charges (approximately $1.50 per title), which will be added to your order. California residents must add sales tax. Quantity discounts available. Allow three weeks delivery time.